THE OFFICIAL
TOTTENHAM HOTSPUR
FOOTBALL CLUB
ANNUAL 2013

Written by Michael Bridge

Designed by Nicky Regan

A Grange Publication

© 2012. Published by Grange Communications Ltd., Edinburgh, under licence from Tottenham Hotspur ltd. Printed in the EU.

Photography © Action Images and Simon Mooney

ISBN: 978-1-908925-15-2

£7.99

CONTENTS

WELCOME

DEAR SUPPORTERS

Welcome to the 2013 Official Tottenham Hotspur Annual.

We are now enjoying a new era under Head Coach Andre-Villas Boas, who is joined by exciting new signings Jan Vertonghen, Gylfi Sigurdsson, Emmanuel Adebayor, Mousa Dembele, Hugo Lloris and Clint Dempsey at White Hart Lane.

The 2011/12 campaign was certainly an eventful season. After finishing fourth in the Barclays Premier League, we were denied our place in the Champions League after Chelsea beat Bayern Munich on penalties in the Final, while we returned to Wembley Stadium for the FA Cup semi-finals.

In the following pages, you'll find a comprehensive 2011/12 season review and an in-depth look into Andre's new regime. Player profiles, along with a quiz section and a review of our Euro 2012 and Olympic stars will leave you with a wealth of Spurs knowledge.

So enjoy the Tottenham Hotspur 2013 Annual.

Come on you Spurs!

Michael Bridge

ARGUABLY THE MOST EXCITING SEASON IN THE PREMIER LEAGUE, TOTTENHAM HOTSPUR FINISHED IN FOURTH FOR THE SECOND TIME IN THREE SEASONS. FOURTH PLACE WOULD USUALLY SEE THE CLUB ENTER THE CHAMPIONS LEAGUE, BUT DUE TO CHELSEA'S CHAMPIONS LEAGUE TRIUMPH, THE CLUB MISSED OUT ON EUROPE'S ELITE COMPETITION IN HEARTBREAKING FASHION. ON THE POSITIVE SIDE, THE TEAM CONTINUED TO IMPRESS HOME AND AWAY AND LED OUR COMPETITORS TO DESCRIBE US AS THE MOST ENTERTAINING SIDE IN THE LEAGUE.

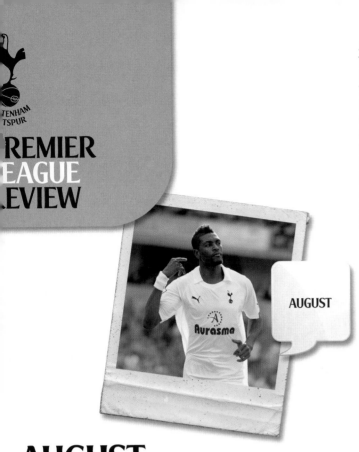

AUGUST

SEPTEMBER

SEPTEMBER WAS A FANTASTIC MONTH. SCOTT PARKER JOINED THE CLUB FROM WEST HAM AND EMMANUEL ADEBAYOR ARRIVED ON LOAN FROM MANCHESTER CITY.

We registered our first points on the board with a 2-0 win away to Wolves. Adebayor with a debut goal and Jermain Defoe adding a second. One of our most impressive performances of the season was a 4-0 win at home to Liverpool. Luka Modric scored an outstanding opening goal. Defoe's goal and two from Adebayor made it a perfect day at White Hart Lane. Our 100% record in September was confirmed with a 2-1 win away to Wigan. Rafael van der Vaart and Gareth Bale were on target for Spurs.

PLD: 3	W: 3	D: 0	L: 0
END OF MONTH POSITION: 6TH			

AUGUST

DUE TO THE TROUBLES IN LONDON, OUR OPENING DAY FIXTURE AGAINST EVERTON WAS POSTPONED.

This meant we started our season with a trip to Old Trafford. After an evenly-contested first half, goals from Danny Welbeck, Anderson and Wayne Rooney gave the Champions all three points. Our difficult start continued with a devastating 5-1 defeat to Manchester City. Edin Dzeko scoring four goals on a forgettable day. Younes Kaboul was on target for Spurs.

PLD: A2	W: 0	D: 0	L: 2
END OF MONTH POSITION:			20TH

SEPTEMBER

OCTOBER

NOVEMBER

OCTOBER

OUR GOOD FORM CONTINUED IN OCTOBER AND WHAT A WAY TO START THE MONTH, WITH A 2-1 WIN OVER OUR NORTH LONDON RIVALS. RAFA VAN DER VAART PUT SPURS AHEAD.

Aaron Ramsey levelled, but a wonder goal from Kyle Walker meant the points were going to the lilywhite half of North London. In-form Newcastle were our next opponents. Rafa's penalty and another from Jermain Defoe put Spurs 2-1 ahead but a late goal from Shola Ameobi earned a point for Newcastle. We secured three more points, this time at Blackburn. Two goals from van der Vaart, one a superb left-footed effort, was enough to earn the win. Our final league match of the month ended in another victory. Two goals from the outstanding Gareth Bale and another from Rafa lifted Spurs up to fifth in the table and placed August very much in the back of our minds.

PLD: 4	W: 3	D: 1	L: 0
END OF MONTH POSITION:		5TH	

NOVEMBER

OUR SUPERB RUN OF FORM CONTINUED IN NOVEMBER WITH MANY PUNDITS CLAIMING OUR FOOTBALL IS THE BEST IN THE PREMIER LEAGUE.

We secured a very impressive 3-1 win at Fulham. A Chris Baird own goal and a superb goal from Aaron Lennon put Spurs 2-0 ahead. Fulham pulled a goal back but Jermain Defoe sealed victory in stoppage time. Emmanuel Adebayor scored both goals as we comfortably defeated Aston Villa at White Hart Lane. Our next match was a tricky trip to West Brom. Despite going down to an early goal we secured all three points with two from Adebayor and Jermain Defoe which gave us our ninth win in 10 league games to lift us up to third.

PLD: 3	W: 3	D: 0	L: 0
END OF MONTH POSITION:		3RD	

DECEMBER

WE STARTED DECEMBER WITH A COMFORTABLE 3-0 WIN AT HOME TO BOLTON. GARETH BALE, JERMAIN DEFOE AND AARON LENNON WERE ALL ON TARGET.

Our first defeat since August came at the Britannia Stadium in a hugely frustrating game. Two goals from Matthew Etherington gave the home side a 2-0 half-time lead. Emmanuel Adebayor replied with a penalty. We took control of the game but couldn't find an equaliser. A number of refereeing decisions went against us to add to our frustration and Kaboul was later sent off for a second yellow to end a miserable and very painful day for Spurs.

With the table tight at the top, it was important to get some points back on the board and we achieved that with a 1-0 win over Sunderland. Roman Pavlyuchenko scored the only goal of the game. London rivals Chelsea were next to arrive at the Lane. Emmanuel Adebayor scored on eight minutes but Daniel Sturridge levelled on 23 minutes to earn the West London side a point. Two days after Christmas, we travelled to Carrow Road where Gareth Bale stole the show with two goals and keeping our impressive run of form in tact. Swansea were our opponents on New Years Eve. Rafa van der Vaart opened the scoring for Spurs but Scott Sinclair levelled with only six minutes remaining. We ended 2011 in third place and headed into the New Year with plenty to look forward to.

PLD: 6	W: 3	D: 2	L: 1
END OF MONTH POSITION:		3RD	

JANUARY

JANUARY

WE STARTED THE NEW YEAR WITH A 1-0 WIN OVER WEST BROM AT WHITE HART LANE, JERMAIN DEFOE WITH THE GOAL.

Everton were next in our rearranged game from the opening day of the season. Aaron Lennon and a wonder strike from Benoit Assou-Ekotto secured a fine victory. We were to suffer a frustrating afternoon in our next home match after being held to a 1-1 draw against Wolves. Luka Modric equalised, but we couldn't find a winner. By now, Spurs were considered genuine title contenders. Our next match at Manchester City was crucial. After a tense and goalless first half, Samir Nasri opened the scoring. Joleon Lescott added a second for the league leaders. Jermain Defoe pulled a goal back then an outstanding goal from Gareth Bale drew Spurs level. Mario Balotelli scored a stoppage time penalty to break Spurs hearts. Our final match of the month kept us in the title race after a comfortable 3-1 win over Wigan. Two goals from Gareth Bale and another from Luka Modric earned victory.

PLD: 5	W: 3	D: 1	L: 1
END OF MONTH POSITION:	3RD		

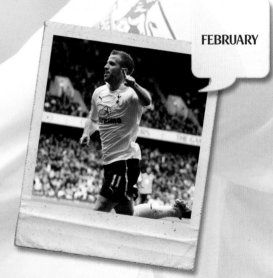

FEBRUARY

FEBRUARY

FEBRUARY STARTED WITH A HARD-FOUGHT DRAW AT LIVERPOOL. HEAVY FOG HAD PUT THE MATCH IN SERIOUS DOUBT BUT WE CAME AWAY HAPPY WITH A POINT.

Our next match was arguably our best performance of the season as we thrashed Newcastle 5-0 at White Hart Lane. Benoit Assou-Ekotto, Louis Saha (2), Emmanuel Adebayor (2) and one from Niko Kranjcar sealed an emphatic win. Delight turned to huge disappointment in our next match after a 5-2 defeat in the North London derby. Saha scored, with Adebayor adding a penalty.

PLD: 3	W: 1	D: 1	L: 1
END OF MONTH POSITION:	3RD		

APRIL

MARCH

WE SUFFERED A 3-1 DEFEAT TO MANCHESTER UNITED IN OUR NEXT MATCH, JERMAIN DEFOE WITH OUR GOAL. OUR POOR RUN OF FORM CONTINUED WITH A 1-0 DEFEAT AT EVERTON.

Rafael van der Vaart scored a late equaliser to secure a point at home to Stoke, but we dropped down to fourth after this result. The race for the Champions League was reaching a crucial stage with Chelsea and Newcastle just behind us in the table. We earned a valuable point at Stamford Bridge in our next match.

PLD: 4	W: 0	D: 2	L: 2
END OF MONTH POSITION:		4TH	

MARCH

APRIL

IN OUR FIRST MATCH IN APRIL, WE ENTERTAINED SWANSEA, A SIDE THAT IMPRESSED EVERYONE UNDER BRENDAN RODGERS IN THEIR FIRST SEASON IN THE PREMIER LEAGUE.

Rafael van der Vaart opened the scoring. Swansea levelled but Emmanuel Adebayor scored twice as we strengthened our position in the top four. We secured a point at Martin O'Neill's Sunderland in our next match. We suffered disappointment two days after as Norwich claimed all three points at White Hart Lane. Our poor run of form continued with a 1-0 defeat at Queens Park Rangers. Goals from van der Vaart and a wonderful free-kick from Kyle Walker secured a crucial three points at home to struggling Blackburn.

PLD: 5	W: 2	D: 1 L	: 2
END OF MONTH POSITION:		4TH	

MAY

MAY

WE TRAVELLED TO BOLTON ON MAY 2ND, KNOWING A WIN WOULD PUT US IN A GREAT POSITION TO CLAIM A TOP FOUR FINISH. GOALS FROM LUKA MODRIC, RAFAEL VAN DER VAART AND TWO FROM EMMANUEL ADEBAYOR SECURED OUR FIRST AWAY WIN IN NINE LEAGUE GAMES.

We were left frustrated at Aston Villa in our final away match of the season. Villa led at half-time and Danny Rose was sent off early in the second half. An Adebayor penalty earned a point, but after dominating, it certainly felt like two points dropped. Our final match of the season was at home to Fulham, knowing we could still secure third place. Adebayor put Spurs ahead on only two minutes. The fans had even more reason to cheer after hearing West Brom had taken a 2-1 lead against Arsenal. Arsenal were able to secure a 3-2 win and, despite a 2-0 win against Fulham, we had to settle for fourth. So, a top four finish secured but while that usually results in celebration, Chelsea's participation in the Champions League Final meant we faced an agonising wait to discover our fate. As we all know now, Chelsea's win on penalties meant we dropped into the Europa League. This disappointment has made the club determined not to suffer similar heartbreak in the future, with major signings and a change of direction in our management structure completed during pre-season.

PLD: 3	W: 2	D: 1	L: 0
FINAL POSITION:			4TH

FINAL PREMIER LEAGUE TABLE 2102

			HOME					AWAY						
		P	W	D	L	F	A	W	D	L	F	A	GD	PTS
1	Man City	38	18	1	0	55	12	10	4	5	38	17	+64	89 (C)
2	Man Utd	38	15	2	2	52	19	13	3	3	37	14	+56	89
3	Arsenal	38	12	4	3	39	17	9	3	7	35	32	+25	70
4	Tottenham Hotspur	38	13	3	3	39	17	7	6	6	27	24	+25	69
5	Newcastle	38	11	5	3	29	17	8	3	8	27	34	+5	65
6	Chelsea	38	12	3	4	41	24	6	7	6	24	22	+19	64
7	Everton	38	10	3	6	28	15	5	8	6	22	25	+10	56
8	Liverpool	38	6	9	4	24	16	8	1	10	23	24	+7	52
9	Fulham	38	10	5	4	36	26	4	5	10	12	25	-3	52
10	West Brom	38	6	3	10	21	22	7	5	7	24	30	-7	47
11	Swansea	38	8	7	4	27	18	4	4	11	17	33	-7	47
12	Norwich	38	7	6	6	28	30	5	5	9	24	36	-14	47
13	Sunderland	38	7	7	5	26	17	4	5	10	19	29	-1	45
14	Stoke	38	7	8	4	25	20	4	4	11	11	33	-17	45
15	Wigan	38	5	7	7	22	27	6	3	10	20	35	-20	43
16	Aston Villa	38	4	7	8	20	25	3	10	6	17	28	-16	38
17	QPR	38	7	5	7	24	25	3	2	14	19	41	-23	37
18	Bolton	38	4	4	11	23	39	6	2	11	23	38	-31	36 (R)
19	Blackburn	38	6	1	12	26	33	2	6	11	22	45	-30	31 (R)
20	Wolves	38	3	3	13	19	43	2	7	10	21	39	-42	25 (R

CARLING CUP
THIRD
ROUND

CARLING CUP THIRD ROUND

A MIXTURE OF YOUTH AND FRINGE PLAYERS TRAVELLED TO THE BRITANNIA STADIUM FOR A DIFFICULT THIRD ROUND TIE.

Thomas Sorensen saved debutant Massimo Luongo's spot-kick to give Stoke a 7-6 win in the shoot-out.

**STOKE CITY 0-0 TOTTENHAM HOTSPUR
(STOKE WIN 7-6 ON PENALTIES)**

FA CUP THIRD ROUND

A packed White Hart Lane crowd witnessed an entertaining third round tie, as Spurs beat League Two side Cheltenham Town. Jermain Defoe, Roman Pavlyuchenko and Giovani Dos Santos with the goals.

TOTTENHAM HOTSPUR 3-0 CHELTENHAM TOWN

FA CUP FOURTH ROUND

We had to survive a second-half onslaught to reach the FA Cup fifth round, but a goal from Rafael van der Vaart on 44 minutes was enough to earn victory.

WATFORD 0-1 TOTTENHAM HOTSPUR

FA CUP FIFTH ROUND

League One side Stevenage secured a deserved replay at White Hart Lane. In a game of very few chances, we thought we had taken the lead but Louis Saha's effort was ruled offside.

STEVENAGE 0-0 TOTTENHAM HOTSPUR

FA CUP FIFTH ROUND REPLAY

We played a full strength side in the replay as we secured our place in the quarter-final. Joel Byrom put Stevenage ahead with a fourth minute penalty. But two goals from Jermain Defoe and a penalty from Emmanuel Adebayor were enough to send us through in front of yet another packed White Hart Lane crowd.

TOTTENHAM HOTSPUR 3-1 STEVENAGE

FA CUP SIXTH ROUND

This was a rearranged quarter-final tie after the original match was abandoned due to Fabrice Muamba suffering a cardiac arrest in the first half. Muamba, 24, was fit enough to walk out of hospital just one month after the ordeal, much to the delight of all football fans around the world. Second-half goals from Ryan Nelsen, Gareth Bale and Louis Saha sent Tottenham into the semi-final of the FA Cup.

TOTTENHAM HOTSPUR 3-1 BOLTON WANDERERS

FA CUP SEMI-FINAL

Our FA Cup run came to an end in controversial fashion. Chelsea were leading through Didier Drogba's goal when Ledley King and Benoit Assou-Ekotto blocked Juan Mata's shot in a frantic goalmouth scramble. Referee Martin Atkinson awarded a goal, despite replays clearly showing the ball didn't cross the line. Gareth Bale pulled a goal back but further strikes from Ramires, Frank Lampard and Florent Malouda sealed Chelsea's place in the final.

TOTTENHAM HOTSPUR 1-5 CHELSEA

TOTTENHAM HOTSPUR

EUROPA LEAGUE REVIEW

UEFA EUROPA LEAGUE PLAY-OFF ROUND 1ST LEG

HEARTS 0-5 TOTTENHAM HOTSPUR

After our opening league fixture against Everton was postponed, our first team squad were selected for this mouth-watering play-off tie. Goals from Rafael van der Vaart, Jermain Defoe, Jake Livermore, Aaron Lennon and Gareth Bale sealed a comfortable win.

UEFA EUROPA LEAGUE PLAY-OFF ROUND 2ND LEG

TOTTENHAM HOTSPUR 0-0 HEARTS

With our group place all but secure after our first leg performance, a number of players from our academy squad were selected for the second leg. Harry Kane missed a penalty, as youngsters Tom Carroll and Ryan Fredericks made their Spurs debuts.

UEFA EUROPA LEAGUE MATCHDAY 1

PAOK 0-0 TOTTENHAM HOTSPUR

Kyle Walker was the only first team regular to make the trip to Greece. PAOK defender Lino missed a first half penalty.

UEFA EUROPA LEAGUE MATCHDAY 2

TOTTENHAM HOTSPUR 3-1 SHAMROCK ROVERS

Shamrock were 40 minutes away from the greatest result in their history after Stephen Rice gave the away side the lead. Roman Pavlyuchenko, Jermain Defoe and Giovani Dos Santos secured a 3-1 win.

ON YOU SPURS THE GAME IS ABOUT GLORY TOTT

UEFA EUROPA LEAGUE MATCHDAY 3

TOTTENHAM HOTSPUR 1-0 RUBIN KAZAN

Roman Pavlyuchenko scored a superb free-kick to put Spurs in a strong position in Group A. We held on for all three points, despite strong pressure from Rubin in the second half.

UEFA EUROPA LEAGUE MATCHDAY 4

RUBIN KAZAN 1-0 TOTTENHAM HOTSPUR

Natcho's second half free-kick sealed victory for Rubin Kazan. In extremely cold conditions in Russia, the home side dominated and deserved their victory.

UEFA EUROPA LEAGUE MATCHDAY 5

TOTTENHAM HOTSPUR 1-2 PAOK

Our hopes of qualification took a huge dent after a surprise home defeat to PAOK. The Greek side raced into a 2-0 lead through a Dimitris Salpingidis header and a Stefanos Athanasiadis tap in. Luka Modric replied with a penalty, but PAOK held on for a famous win.

UEFA EUROPA LEAGUE MATCHDAY 6

SHAMROCK ROVERS 0-4 TOTTENHAM HOTSPUR

Our participation in the Europa League came to an end despite thrashing Shamrock. Steven Pienaar, Andros Townsend, Jermain Defoe and Harry Kane were our goalscorers. Our European adventure came to an end for another year. Despite the disappointment of our exit, a number of players gained great experience during the tournament which bodes well for their futures at the club.

GARETH BALE

At only 23 years of age, Gareth Bale is an experienced member of the Tottenham Hotspur squad. The 2011 PFA Player of the Year enjoyed another successful season. The Welsh international finished the campaign with 12 goals from 40 appearances in all competitions and an impressive nine in 34 matches in the Premier League. At the end of the season, Gareth signed a new four-year contract, committing his future to the Club until 2016.

The popular left-sided player's performances over recent seasons have attracted worldwide acclaim and have seen him named in the PFA Premier League Team of the Year in the past two seasons, as well as the UEFA Team of the Year, during our Champions League campaign. Despite interest from clubs all around Europe, Gareth had no hesitation in signing a new deal. "I've been here for five years now and I've enjoyed every minute. The fans have been great to me and I'd love to re-pay them and do the very best for them. The Club is progressing and I want to be a part of that, so it was good to get the deal done.

"I love the Club and the fans and I want to play my part in trying to get us back into the Champions League - where we belong. We've a good, young squad and we need to work together to get back on the biggest stage again."

Gareth set Europe alight in the Champions League, notably against Inter Milan, scoring an amazing hat-trick in the San Siro. Gareth's threat on the left hand side often leads to clubs marking him with two players. He's a marked man now that's for sure. Last season Gareth would often move into the centre of the pitch and with his pace, he's a real problem for central defenders. In the club's 2012 US tour, Gareth played as a central striker and his strength and ability in the air caused problems for the defence. There's little doubt his main threat comes from the left hand side, but his versatility will he a huge asset to Spurs. "Last season I was getting double and treble-marked on the wing, so I was able to come inside and score a few goals in more central areas. Now it's a case of mixing it all up and putting my whole game together. Hopefully I'll score more goals next season. I did quite well with my assists last season, but I'd like to improve that as well. I'm looking at my all-round game, trying new things and trying to be the best player I can be."

Despite his amazing ability, Gareth is looking to improve as a player over the next few years. "I know I'm getting better and my aim is to be as good as I can be. I'm still young, 23, still learning and this is the right place for me to keep progressing as a player. Definitely, there is a lot more to come."

GARETH BALE

BALE FACTFILE

Born: July 16, 1989

Joined Spurs May 2007

PFA Player of the Season, 2011

UEFA Team of the Year, 2011

Previous Club(s): Southampton

11

KYLE
WALKER

28

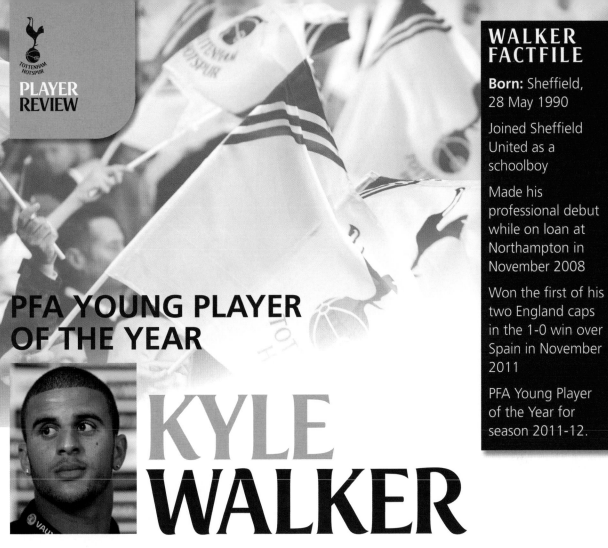

PFA YOUNG PLAYER OF THE YEAR

KYLE WALKER

Kyle Walker enjoyed an outstanding first full season at Tottenham Hotspur, winning the PFA Young Player of the Year Award.

The flying full-back played more games than anyone else – making 47 appearances and 45 starts of our 53 matches in all competitions – scored his first two goals for us (both Goal of the Month winners) and made his full England debut, including a Man of the Match performance against Sweden.

Kyle became the first Spurs player to win the award since Glenn Hoddle in 1980, beating the likes of Sergio Aguero, Danny Welbeck, Daniel Sturridge and our very own Gareth Bale to the honour. He was also named in the PFA's Premier League Team of the Season and his strike against Arsenal won Supporters Clubs Goal of the Season. By now, Kyle was a certainty for the European Championships in Poland and the Ukraine. Sadly, a toe injury forced him to miss Euro 2012, but thankfully he fully recovered ahead of a big year for the former Sheffield United defender.

Despite an amazing first season at White Hart Lane, Kyle typically played down his achievements. "On a personal level, it's been fantastic. It's been a dream. I've experienced highs, lows, the good and bad.

It's been a massive learning curve for me. I can't wait for the next few seasons here, where I hope to improve even more."

After very successful loan spells at Queens Park Rangers and Aston Villa, Kyle's reputation soared nationally, but after a superb first season at Tottenham, he's now a key player for club and country, and teammate Gareth Bale says Kyle will be a marked man from now on.

"He needed a run in the team, he got that and he showed exactly what he could do last season. Players know all about him now, they will be looking to stop those forward runs and he has to find a way around it – I'm sure he will."

It didn't take Kyle long to become a White Hart Lane hero. After scoring the winning goal against Arsenal, he quickly realised just how important that goal was to the Spurs supporters. "It was a great feeling, my first North London derby and hopefully there will be many more derbies and goals to come," said Kyle.

Kyle will have many more opportunities to score against Arsenal, after signing a new contract that will keep him at White Hart Lane until 2017. "My future is at this club. I believe we're on the brink of something really big, and I want to be part of that."

MANAGER
PROFILE

"It's a massive opportunity for me and I'm extremely privileged to be working here"

Andre Villas-Boas was appointed Tottenham Hotspur Head Coach on July 3rd. The former FC Porto and Chelsea Boss was the stand-out candidate as Chairman Daniel Levy looked ahead to a new era at White Hart Lane.

At 34, you would think Andre Villas-Boas was a rookie at managerial level, but he's already experienced plenty of ups and downs. A successful playing career never really materialised, but his interest in management came at a very early age. Sir Bobby Robson recognised Andre's natural talent for scouting and coaching players, which earned him a role in the Porto youth set-up. He was awarded the UEFA coaching C licence at the age of just 17. At only 21, Andre became Manager of the British Virgin Islands. He then moved back to Porto to take charge of the Under-19 side. He picked up his B and A licences and would later be promoted to study under Jose Mourinho as his assistant. Andre quickly became a key member of Mourinho's coaching staff, following him to Chelsea and Inter Milan, winning numerous trophies.

Andre was now ready to become a number one.

His first club managerial role was in his native Portugal, taking Academica de Coimbra to a very respectable 11th place. He then joined the club where it all started – FC Porto. His one season was a dream come true, winning all four trophies including an unbeaten league title. And after winning the UEFA Europa League, Andre was now the most in-demand coach in world football. This amazing success saw him take over at Chelsea in June 2011, and he extended his own personal undefeated League record to 39 games, before leaving the post the following March. Villas-Boas was not out of work for long though, with Spurs calling on him to lead a new era at the club ahead of the 2012-13 season.

"It's a massive opportunity for me and I'm extremely privileged to be working here", said Andre.

"It was important for me to choose somewhere where I am surrounded by the right commitment and the right people and I have found it."

"It's fantastic to come to a club with such high expectations of the future and I want to respond to the trust that the Chairman has put in me, with success."

23

PLAYER PROFILES 2012/13

Holder of the record for most consecutive starts in the Premier League, Brad enjoyed a super-consistent first season at White Hart Lane in 2011-12.

Brad's incredible run of starts reached the 300 mark at QPR in April and he was presented a special Barclays Merit Award in recognition. He took his tally to 304 matches by the end of the season when he achieved another record – becoming the Club's oldest player at 40 years, 350 days, passing the mark set by Jimmy Cantrell that had stood for 89 years.

 @Friedel_B

CARLO CUDICINI

HEURELHO GOMES

Carlo joined Spurs from Chelsea in January 2009.

He has provided strong competition for the number one jersey. The Italian was our number one during our FA Cup and Europa League campaigns.

Popular goalkeeper, capable of making almost impossible saves, Gomes joined us in the summer of 2008.

The arrival and performances of Brad Friedel restricted the Brazilian international to just four starts in 2011-12, three in the Europa League.

BRAD FRIEDEL

HUGO LLORIS

STEVEN CAULKER

Arguably Tottenham's most improved player. The powerful centre-back is now rated as one of the best in the Premier League.

The French international played 33 of 38 matches as we finished fourth in the Premier League in 2011-12 and made a huge contribution to a defence that kept 14 clean sheets – our best in the Premier League, and also since 1986-87. He played seven times in cup competition.

 @YounsKabs4

The France international captain began his senior playing career with Nice in 2005.

He made 72 appearances before departing for French champions Olympique Lyonnais, where he clocked up 146 league appearances, twice winning the Ligue 1 Goalkeeper of the Year award.

Steven enjoyed a great campaign on loan at Swansea City last season.

His form earned him a place in Great Britain's Olympic squad. An England Under-21 regular, Steven made his Spurs debut against Arsenal in the Carling Cup in September, 2010.

YOUNES KABOUL

MICHAEL DAWSON

JAN VERTONGHEN

KYLE WALKER

Dawson endured a difficult and injury-hit 2011-12.

'Daws' was restricted to just 13 appearances in all competitions – and just six starts in the Premier League – first by Achilles trouble and then an ankle injury. The England international is one of the most popular players at the club and, when fit, is a top class central defender.

Jan joined the club in July from Dutch giants, Ajax.

The Belgium international was named player of the year in the Dutch top flight last season. Jan has scored an incredible 23 goals from central defence. Despite offers from several top clubs, Jan insisted the only club he wanted to sign for was Spurs.

@Jan_Vertonghen

Young, flying full-back Kyle enjoyed a superb season at White Hart Lane, picking up the PFA Young Player of the Year award.

Kyle also won the Spurs Goal of the Season award after his long-range effort against Arsenal. The England international started 37 of our 38 matches in the Premier League and missed just six of 53 in all competitions.

@kyle28walker

DANNY ROSE

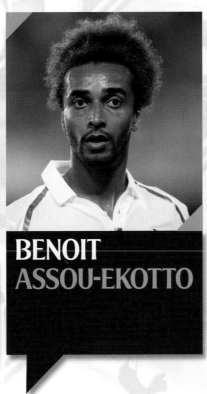

BENOIT ASSOU-EKOTTO

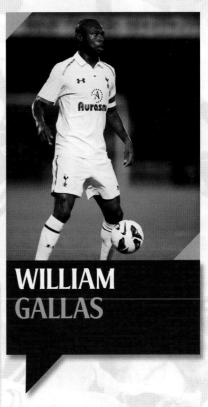

WILLIAM GALLAS

The young midfielder represented Great Britain during the London 2012 Olympic Games.

Danny is often used at left-back in the absence of Benoit Assou-Ekotto and his versatility makes him an useful squad player. Danny is currently on a season-long loan at Sunderland.

Benoit is regarded as one of the top left-backs in the Premier League.

The Cameroon international dislocated his shoulder at QPR in April, 2012 and that meant he missed our last four PL matches, having played in all 34 up to then. He made another six appearances in cup competition. Benoit scored two goals last season, one a 30-yard screamer against Everton.

@Assouekotto

The experienced French defender is now in his third year at the club.

Unfortunately, William was restricted to 15 appearances in the Premier League and 18 in all competitions by nagging calf injuries that meant he had to wait until November for his first match of 2011-12, a Europa League tie at Rubin Kazan.

PLAYER PROFILES 2012/13

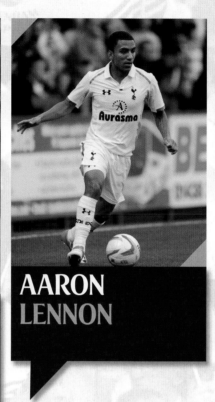

TOM HUDDLESTONE

AARON LENNON

JERMAINE JENAS

A career highlight was captaining the side when we beat Inter Milan 3-1 at White Hart Lane in the Champions League.

A serious ankle injury restricted Tom to only three matches last season but there is no doubt that when fit he is a key member of the squad. Tom has also been capped by England on three occasions.

Aaron featured in 23 league matches for Spurs last season.

The flying winger scored one of the goals of the season against Fulham at Craven Cottage. When fit, Aaron is one of the most dangerous wingers in the Premier League.

This is Jermaine's eighth season at the club and he is now one of the longest-serving players.

Last season Jermaine suffered a serious Achilles injury, ruling him out for the season. Now fully fit, he hopes to force his way into our first XI again.

 **@jjenas8**

@TomHuddlestone6

SANDRO

SCOTT PARKER

GYLFI SIGURDSSON

The Brazilian international is a key member of the Spurs side.

After impressing for Brazil in the London 2012 Olympics, the 23-year-old returned to do what he does best – covering every blade of grass, breaking play up and making bursting runs. A popular member of the squad with huge potential.

 **@sandroraniere**

Scott joined Spurs from West Ham on deadline day in August 2011.

He went on to win the Player of the Year award after a superb season at White Hart Lane. His great performances earned him a place in the Euro 2012 finals.

Our first summer signing. Gylfi is a goalscoring midfielder with a great eye for a pass.

The 22-year-old scored seven goals in 18 games during a very successful loan spell at Swansea City.

PLAYER
PROFILES
2012/13

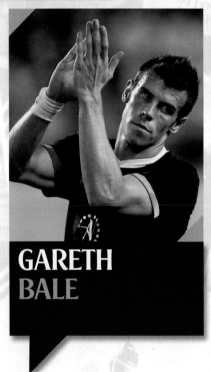

GARETH
BALE

JAKE
LIVERMORE

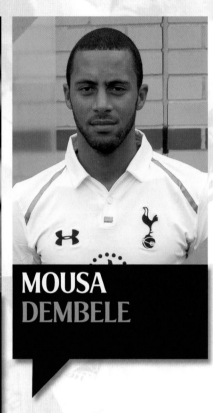

MOUSA
DEMBELE

The powerful left-sided Welsh international is currently regarded as one of the best young players in European football.

Gareth scored 12 goals in 42 games last season. In July 2012, Bale signed a new four year contract, committing his future to the club until 2016.

After numerous loan spells, Jake finally broke into the first team last season and impressed the supporters with his tenacity in midfield.

Jake scored his first senior goal for Spurs against Hearts in the Europa League last season. Jake won his first England cap against Italy in August 2012.

@29_JL

Skilful attacking midfielder Mousa joined us from Fulham in August, 2012.

The Belgium international has won many admirers with his performances in the Premier League since arriving at Craven Cottage in August 2010 from AZ Alkmaar, with who he won the Eredivisie league title in 2009. Mousa scored on his debut against Norwich.

@mousadembele

JERMAIN DEFOE

EMMANUEL ADEBAYOR

CLINT DEMPSEY

Jermain scored 17 goals last season. From the start or off the bench, Jermain remains one of the most dangerous strikers in the Premier League.

He made a substitute appearance against France in EURO 2012. Jermain became only the 16th player in the Club's history to score 100 goals for Spurs when he hit a screamer against West Brom at the Lane in April, 2011.

@IAmJermainDefoe

The popular Togo striker impressed during his loan at White Hart Lane last season, finishing as our top goalscorer with 18 goals in 37 appearances.

Emmanuel originally moved to England with Arsenal in January, 2006 before joining Manchester City two-and-a-half years later and also enjoyed a spell on loan with Real Madrid in 2011.

Clint joined the club from Fulham on the final day of the summer transfer window.

The attacking midfielder's standout performances for the Cottagers have seen him named their Player of the Season in both the last two seasons and he is also their all-time leading scorer in the Premier League. In total, Dempsey made a total of 224 appearances for Fulham, scoring 60 goals.

Walker's wonder strike wins the North London derby!

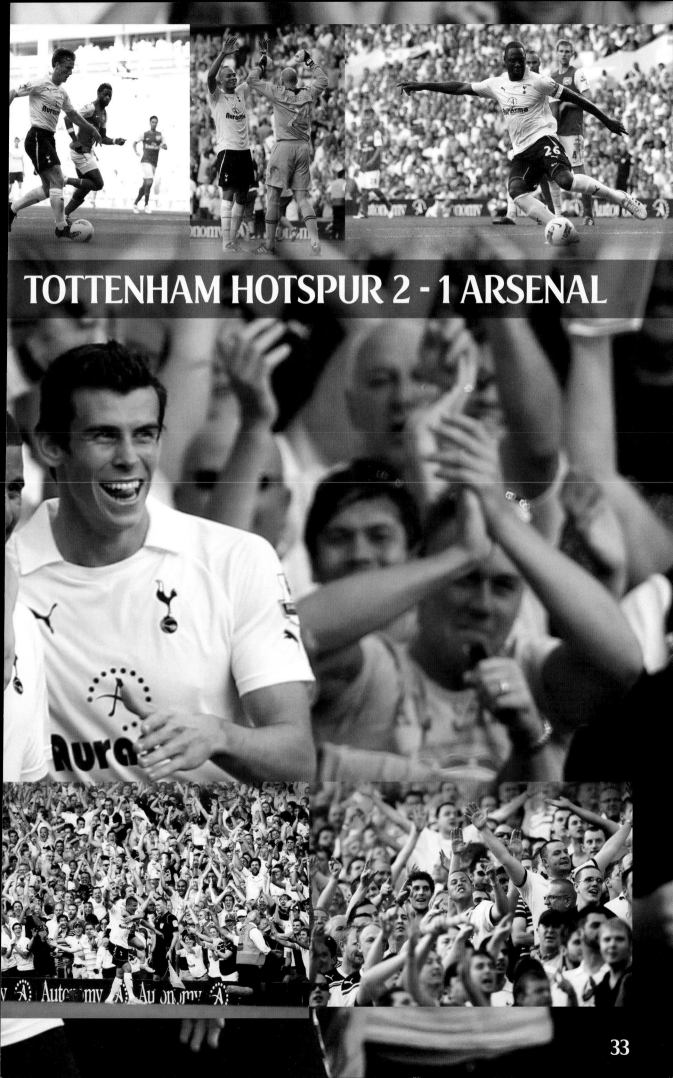

TOTTENHAM HOTSPUR 2 - 1 ARSENAL

JAKE LIVERMORE

What an amazing 12 months for Jake Livermore. In the summer of 2011, there was a strong possibility Jake would be sent out on loan to gain more first team experience.

However, due to injuries to Sandro and Tom Huddlestone, Jake found himself starting in our opening game of the season, away to Manchester United. He didn't look back after that and enjoyed an impressive season at White Hart Lane.

Jake scored his first competitive senior goal for Spurs against Hearts in the Europa League. However, one goal he'll never forget came in a pre-season tournament against Barcelona at Wembley Stadium in July 2009. Loan moves to Derby County, Peterborough, Ipswich and Leeds followed. Despite the invaluable experience, Jake did wonder if and when his first team debut would ever arrive. "Playing competitive league football was important for me, but my dream was always to play for Spurs. It's an amazing club, the one I love. There is so much talent here you're fighting every day to be part of the side."

Season 2011/12 was the big breakthrough year for Jake, who impressed many with his dominant displays in the middle of the park, and while his experience on loan had made him the player he is today, he was delighted to stay at the club last season. "Going on loan is important for young players but I want to play for Spurs. Walking out at White Hart Lane is a great feeling. It's my local club."

Jake featured in every pre-season match under Andre Villas-Boas. Shortly after returning home from our final pre-season match in Valencia, he received news all players dream about – an England call-up. Jake earned his first cap against Italy, a reward for all the hard work and determination from the midfielder. "I couldn't believe it at first. I never even thought about England. Being involved at Spurs was the only thing on my mind so to hear of the call-up was a shock. I loved the experience and hope to be involved again in the future."

And if Jake continues with the form he has shown over the past year, it's bound to be the first of many caps.

LIVERMORE FACTFILE

Born: November 14, 1989

Position: Midfielder

Joined Spurs Academy, 2006

Previous Club(s): Milton Keynes Dons (loan), Crewe Alexandra (loan), Derby County (loan), Peterborough United (loan), Ipswich Town (loan), Leeds United (loan)

JAKE
LIVERMORE

29

35

2011/12 TOTTENHAM HOTSPUR PLAYER OF THE YEAR

When Scott Parker signed at the end of the 2011 summer transfer window, few knew just how much of an impact the midfielder would have on the team.

A great season saw him earn a place in Roy Hodgson's Euro 2012 squad, playing all three group games and the quarter-final.

Scott made his debut against Wolves – our third league match of the season. We won 2-0 and went on an 11 match unbeaten run. With injuries to Sandro and Tom Huddlestone, Scott's signing came at a perfect time. Alongside playmaker Luka Modric, Scott added bite and strength in midfield.

"I think I complemented the team well and at the same time, the players have complemented me. I feel I've fitted in really well and I'm really pleased with how it's gone.

"When you come to a new club, the one thing you want to do is settle in really well, and quickly, hitting the ground running. I felt I did that."

Scott certainly did hit the ground running, winning our Player of the Month awards for September, October and November. Amazingly, he won the award again in January and February.

International recognition came too, as he was voted England's Player of the Year for 2011. Then, Scott received the ultimate honour – captaining England against The Netherlands at Wembley. In total, Scott played 34 games in the Premier League and FA Cup in his first season, starting 33 times.

Scott's experience had a positive effect on the squad. Despite playing in a similar position, Jake Livermore believes the signing of Parker helped his game last season. "Obviously Scott coming here added competition," reflected Jake. "However, I think it's made me a better player, staying here, learning from him and playing alongside him.

"He's taught me all about the timing of closing down, the timing of pressing and when to sit off and get into shape. They're little things you pick up on, little things that perhaps you can't put your finger on and explain, but training with him and all the other players as well, day-in day-out, is the best education possible."

Now working under Head Coach Andre Villas-Boas, Scott's experience is crucial to a young and talented squad. With the retirement of Ledley King, Scott's leadership will play a big part in any potential success in 2013, and if he can replicate the form shown in 2011/12, success for this exciting squad is only around the corner.

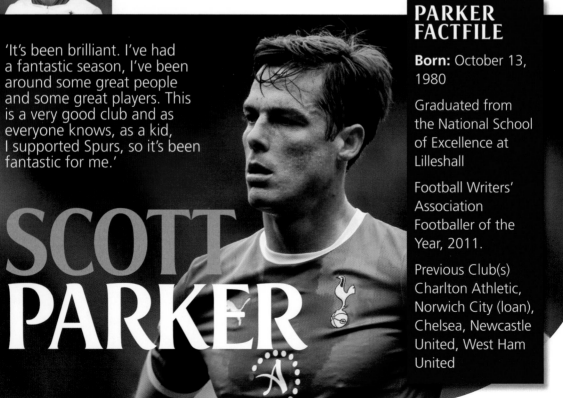

'It's been brilliant. I've had a fantastic season, I've been around some great people and some great players. This is a very good club and as everyone knows, as a kid, I supported Spurs, so it's been fantastic for me.'

SCOTT PARKER

PARKER FACTFILE

Born: October 13, 1980

Graduated from the National School of Excellence at Lilleshall

Football Writers' Association Footballer of the Year, 2011.

Previous Club(s) Charlton Athletic, Norwich City (loan), Chelsea, Newcastle United, West Ham United

WORD SEARCH

Bale

Defoe

Friedel

Kaboul

Lennon

Parker

Sandro

Sigurdsson

Vertonghen

Walker

L	L	R	T	D	E	F	O	E	K	P	N
K	R	T	Q	R	Y	F	L	X	A	F	O
V	L	R	T	T	R	A	N	G	B	T	S
T	E	F	E	I	B	O	P	R	O	Z	S
V	X	R	E	K	N	Y	Y	O	U	V	D
Y	V	D	T	N	L	W	N	R	L	F	R
Y	E	L	E	O	L	A	G	D	T	P	U
L	Z	L	C	M	N	C	W	N	L	D	G
Y	F	K	C	Q	K	G	B	A	P	Q	I
D	R	E	K	R	A	P	H	S	N	T	S
T	W	Q	P	W	M	M	M	K	E	L	L
F	N	B	K	N	N	M	R	M	N	K	L

'I've joined a massive club with fantastic players.'

GYLFI SIGURDSSON

Gylfi Sigurdsson became our first signing under Andre Villas-Boas. The attacking midfielder is no stranger to the Premier League having enjoyed an impressive loan spell at Swansea City during the second half of last season.

The 23-year old attracted attention from several clubs after his loan at Swansea. During his time at the Liberty Stadium, he scored seven times in 19 appearances as well as picking up the Barclays Player of the Month award for March. Sigurdsson decided to join Tottenham, and the Icelandic international made it clear the decision was not a difficult one.

"It's a massive club with fantastic players. The main target at Swansea was to stay in the league. Here at Spurs, it's a big club and we aim to win titles and silverware," Sigurdsson said.

Sigurdsson first impressed at Reading, scoring 20 goals in 42 games from midfield. His impressive form for Reading earned him a move to German big spenders Hoffenheim. In May 2011, Gylfi was voted Hoffenheim's fans' player of the season, despite only starting 13 games. Unable to settle in Germany, Gylfi returned to England, where he enjoyed an impressive loan spell at Swansea. Sigurdsson says he's learned a lot from his time at Reading and Swansea, which is good news for a Spurs side that has lacked goals from central midfield.

"I've loved my time at Spurs so far. They are a very popular club in Iceland and I know many fans back home will be watching me this season. Everything is perfect for me. The fans have been great, the players and of course, the coach. I'm very happy."

'Spurs is one of the biggest clubs in the Premier League and that's one of the reasons I wanted to move here.'

VERTONGHEN FACTFILE

Born: 24 April, 1987 in Belgium

Position: Defender

Former Clubs: Ajax, Waalwijk (loan)

Total club matches before Spurs: 155

Goals: 23

Jan Vertonghen finally completed his move to Spurs in July. Despite interest from clubs from all around Europe, Jan made it clear he only wanted to join Spurs.

The Belgian international defender, snapped-up from Ajax, is already loving life at White Hart Lane and is looking forward to a long career in England.

Jan is a regular in the exciting Belgian international side, he joined Ajax's famed academy in 2003 before signing professional terms in 2006. He went on to play over 200 times in all competitions for Ajax, landing the title in 2011 and 2012 and gaining a wealth of experience in Europe. A regular captain of the team, Jan was also named the prestigious Dutch Player of the Year in 2012. He is an exciting defender who has scored an incredible 23 goals in 15 games.

Once the deal was completed, the central defender said, "I'm delighted to be here, Spurs is a very big club in England. They finished top four a few times and for me,

it's one of the biggest clubs in the Premier League and that's one of the reasons I wanted to move here."

It didn't take long for Jan to settle in at Spurs. His first impression of the squad was one of great harmony. "I only knew Rafa (van der Vaart) but he was still on holiday when I started here. The boys were great and I can say the atmosphere here is wonderful. I spoke to Rafa about Spurs and it was very positive. He gave me a great feeling about the club, the players and the Premier League."

Jan's leadership will be vital, as we look ahead to a big year domestically and in Europe. He's convinced this squad can be successful in 2013. "Spurs were very unlucky last season. They were very close to the top for a very long time. I want to make the team better, that's what I am here for. We have to try and finish as high as possible. The Champions League is a nice target for us, which I believe was the same last season.

We have to try and achieve these goals again."

JAN VERTONGHEN

You're the star!

ONLY JUNIOR MEMBERS CAN BE CHOSEN AS A MASCOT

10 GREAT REASONS TO STAR AS A JUNIOR MEMBER:

- Exclusive **GOODIES** packs
- **TICKET** priority and discounts
- **FREE** stadium tour (worth £9)
- **WIN** invitation to Christmas party with players
- Chance to **STAR** in the new squad photo
- Chance to **MEET** the players
- Chance to **INTERVIEW** a player
- Chance to present Player of the Season **TROPHY**
- Birthday and Christmas **CARDS**
- Junior **MAGAZINES**

EXCLUSIVE TO JUNIOR MEMBERS

BE A PART OF THE TEAM!
BECOME A ONE HOTSPUR JUNIOR MEMBER:

01 **Visit:** tottenhamhotspur.com/juniors
02 **Call:** 0844 8440102

STEFFEN FREUND

GET TO KNOW THE REST OF HEAD COACH ANDRE VILLAS-BOAS' COACHING TEAM

FIRST TEAM FITNESS COACH
Jose Mario Rocha *(pictured last on right)*

Jose has 19 years of experience working in the professional game, the first 17 of those in the set-up at Porto where he was employed as a general coach. It included a spell at Padronese FC, a club whose youth team is effectively the Porto youth second 11.

HEAD OF OPPOSITION SCOUTING
Daniel Sousa *(pictured 2nd on left)*

A knee injury ended Daniel's playing career. Retirement led to him studying sports science and he is now an important member of Andre's backroom team.

FIRST TEAM COACH
Luis Martins *(pictured 2nd from right)*

Luis has previously worked at Sporting Lisbon, where he oversaw the Under 17 and Under 19 sides and was also the club's assistant coach in 2004-05, and Braga. Luis also had a successful coaching spell with Saudi Arabia.

GOALKEEPING COACH
Tony Parks *(pictured 1st on left)*

Tony needs no introduction. Saving the penalty to win the 1984 UEFA Cup, Tony is a Spurs legend.

Steffen Freund returned to Spurs as Assistant Head Coach to Andre Villas-Boas. The popular German couldn't hide his delight when his appointment was officially announced.

Steffen is a Hall of Fame inductee and played for Spurs between 1999 and 2003. The popular coach spent four years at the German FA and went on to coach an impressive German Under-17 side. Steffen is delighted with his new role at the club he loves. "It's a dream to return to Spurs. The philosophy of the youth teams in Germany is exactly the same as at Spurs – play well, be strong with the ball, dominate games and be strong and solid without the ball. White Hart Lane was my living room, from 1999 to 2003. I came back a few times. I'm in the Hall of Fame of this fantastic club and now I'm back in a different role, as coach. That was my dream when I started my B License five, six years ago."

**SPURS
AT EURO
2012**

SPURS AT
EURO 2012

Scott Parker and Jermain Defoe
featured in the 2012
European Championships.

Scott started every match for England,
who were eliminated by Italy on penalties
in the quarter-final. Jermain featured once
against France.

42

SPURS AT THE 2012 OLYMPICS

The London 2012 Olympics has been described as one of the greatest events of all time, and rightly so.

With Team GB winning 29 gold, 17 silver and 19 bronze medals, we finished 3rd in the table – our most successful Olympics for 104 years.

There were also medals for two Spurs players. Giovani dos Santos took Olympic gold and Sandro claimed a silver medal as Mexico beat Brazil 2-1 in the final at Wembley.

We also had Steven Caulker and Danny Rose included in the Great Britain team, Caulker impressing to such an extent he received an England call-up from manager Roy Hodgson.

43

"For me, he's one of the best players I've ever played with and without the injuries, I think he could have been the best centre-half in the world. We always used to say he's not human! He didn't train all week and played 90 minutes on the Saturday. The way he performed with his injuries was nothing short of unbelievable."

**Gareth Bale,
Team-mate 2007-2012**

LEDLEY KING

In July, the Club announced that one of its greatest players, Ledley King, has, as a result of injury, been forced to retire from the game.

Far from departing the Club though, Ledley will be involved in a wide-ranging ambassadorial role and be a champion for the regeneration of Tottenham.

Ledley was our Club Captain. At 31, he is one of a rare breed in modern football, being a one-club man, joining up at the age of 14 before progressing through the ranks to First Team football and subsequently becoming skipper.

"I have been here since I was a boy, I have always considered it my Club and have always found it hard to imagine wearing the shirt of another team," reflected Ledley. "I know that being a one-club man is a rarity these days, but I have always enjoyed being part of the set-up here and the challenge of putting this Club up with the elite where it should be."

Ledley turned professional in July 1998 and made his senior debut under a year later in May 1999 against Liverpool at Anfield. He made 323 First Team appearances in our colours, scoring 14 goals.

Notable high points came with the lifting of the Carling Cup in 2008 after victory over Chelsea at Wembley, with Ledley steering the team to Champions League qualification for the first time in our history in season 2009-10.

His performances for the Club were recognised on the international front and he made his England debut against Italy in March 2002. Ledley won 21 international caps in total and appeared in both the 2004 European Championships and the 2010 World Cup.

Ledley's injury problems were well documented. Being able to play in the Premier League, yet unable to train, took its toll on the classy defender. His eye for reading the game made him one of the best of his generation. Ledley's pace always made him a tough opponent for strikers. Who can forget his sensational tackle on Arjen Robben when the Dutchman was one-on-one with the goalkeeper. Ledley will be remembered for being a top class central defender, but his versatility often saw him play in central midfield in the early stages of his career. Past England Managers, particularly Sven Goran Eriksson and Fabio Capello, were huge admirers of Ledley and were keen to include him in major tournaments despite his injuries.

An ambassadorial role awaits at White Hart Lane for Ledley King. Many will wonder what could have been if he hadn't suffered with his injuries. Spurs fans will remember what was – a true legend, who will never be forgotten.

SUPER SPURS QUIZ

It's a grand old team to play for and it's a grand old team to see, so if you know your history, try this 2013 Super Size Spurs Quiz!

1. Where did Spurs finish last season?

2. Paul Gascoigne joined Spurs from which club?

3. Gylfi Sigurdsson represents which nation?

4. Name our matchday club mascot.

5. Name our opponents in Group A of last season's Europa League.

6. Who was our top goalscorer last season?

7. Who were our opponents in the 1991 FA Cup Final?

8. Who are our new kit manufacturers?

9. What was the first European trophy Spurs won?

10. Name our Assistant Head Coach who is in our Hall of Fame?

11. We signed Scott Parker from which Premier League club?

12. Who scored our Goal of the Season against Arsenal in 2011/12?

13. On how many occasions have Spurs won the League Cup?

14. We signed Jan Vertonghen from which Dutch club?

15. Who did we face on the opening day this season?

SPURS EUROPA STARS

PRE-SEASON REPORT

PRE-SEASON REPORT

STEVENAGE 0-2 TOTTENHAM HOTSPUR

Gylfi Sigurdsson marked his debut with a goal as we beat Stevenage 2-0 in our first pre-season friendly of the summer. Yago Falque scored a second two minutes from time.

LA GALAXY 1-1 TOTTENHAM HOTSPUR

Gareth Bale was outstanding on our tour of America. In the first match, Bale opened the scoring. David Lopes earned LA Galaxy a draw.

TOTTENHAM HOTSPUR 0-0 LIVERPOOL

The second friendly of our pre-season tour of the US ended in a goalless draw against Liverpool in the heat of Baltimore.

Chances were few and far between as temperatures pushed the 100F mark at the M&T Bank Stadium, home of NFL giants Baltimore Ravens.

NEW YORK RED BULLS 1-2 TOTTENHAM HOTSPUR

Two excellent goals in the space of five minutes in the second half secured a deserved win against New York Red Bulls in the Barclays New York Cup.

Trailing 1-0 at half-time despite dominating the first half, Gareth Bale and Gylfi Sigurdsson struck in the 59th and 64th minutes respectively to make the scoreline more reflective of the action in the third and final friendly of our US tour.

WATFORD 0-1 TOTTENHAM HOTSPUR

We returned to England to play Gianfranco Zola's Watford. Jermain Defoe scored a second half header after good work from Kyle Walker.

VALENCIA 2-0 TOTTENHAM HOTSPUR

A fine performance in the Mestalla went unrewarded as two clinical finishes handed Valencia a 2-0 win. Valencia took the lead with an absolute bolt out of the blue from Jonas on 18 minutes.

The second half saw fewer chances but we were the team pushing on when Valencia struck again through Sofianne Feghouli on 76 minutes.

53

GOAL OF THE SEASON

A late contender was Luka Modric's goal at Bolton in May – a key opening goal in a match we had to win. Luka controlled Rafael van der Vaart's angled corner and volleyed an arrow of a shot into the top corner, paving the way for a 4-1 win.

What a season we experienced for outstanding goals! Kyle Walker's superb strike against Arsenal at White Hart Lane won the award for Goal of the Season, as voted for by Spurs fans on our official Facebook page.

The full-back's 30-yard belter, which sealed victory in the first North London Derby of the season, received 3,123 votes and won the contest comfortably. It was Kyle's first goal for Spurs and it couldn't have been better - a fierce drive that swerved late away from Wojciech Szczesny and flew into the bottom corner.

Luka Modric's stunning goal against Liverpool at the start of our Premier League campaign came in second place, and Kyle rounded off the top three with his incredible free-kick scored against Blackburn in April.

There were plenty more stunning goals during the season. Gareth Bale's second goal at Norwich certainly deserves a mention. Luka Modric sent Gareth racing through the middle and he sprinted past two defenders and at full pace, flicked the ball over the advancing John Ruddy to secure a 2-0 win. His goal at Manchester City one month later was even better. Aaron Lennon drove down the left, cut in and rolled the ball to the Welshman, who hit a first-time curler across and over Joe Hart into the far corner.

55

SEASON
REVIEW

Barclays Premier League

Position	Team	P	W	D	L	F	A	GD	Pts
1	Man City	38	28	5	5	93	29	64	89C
2	Man Utd	38	28	5	5	89	33	56	89
3	Arsenal	38	21	7	10	74	49	25	70
4	Tottenham Hotspur	38	20	9	9	66	41	25	69
5	Newcastle	38	19	8	11	56	51	5	65
6	Chelsea	38	18	10	10	65	46	19	64
7	Everton	38	15	11	12	50	40	10	56
8	Liverpool	38	14	10	14	47	40	7	52
9	Fulham	38	14	10	14	48	51	-3	52
10	West Brom	38	13	8	17	45	52	-7	47
11	Swansea	38	12	11	15	44	51	-7	47
12	Norwich	38	12	11	15	52	66	-14	47
13	Sunderland	38	11	12	15	45	46	-1	45
14	Stoke	38	11	12	15	36	53	-17	45
15	Wigan	38	11	10	17	42	62	-20	43
16	Aston Villa	38	7	17	14	37	53	-16	38
17	QPR	38	10	7	21	42	65	-23	37
18	Bolton	38	10	6	22	46	77	-31	36R
19	Blackburn	38	8	7	23	48	78	-30	31R
20	Wolves	38	5	10	23	40	82	-42	25R

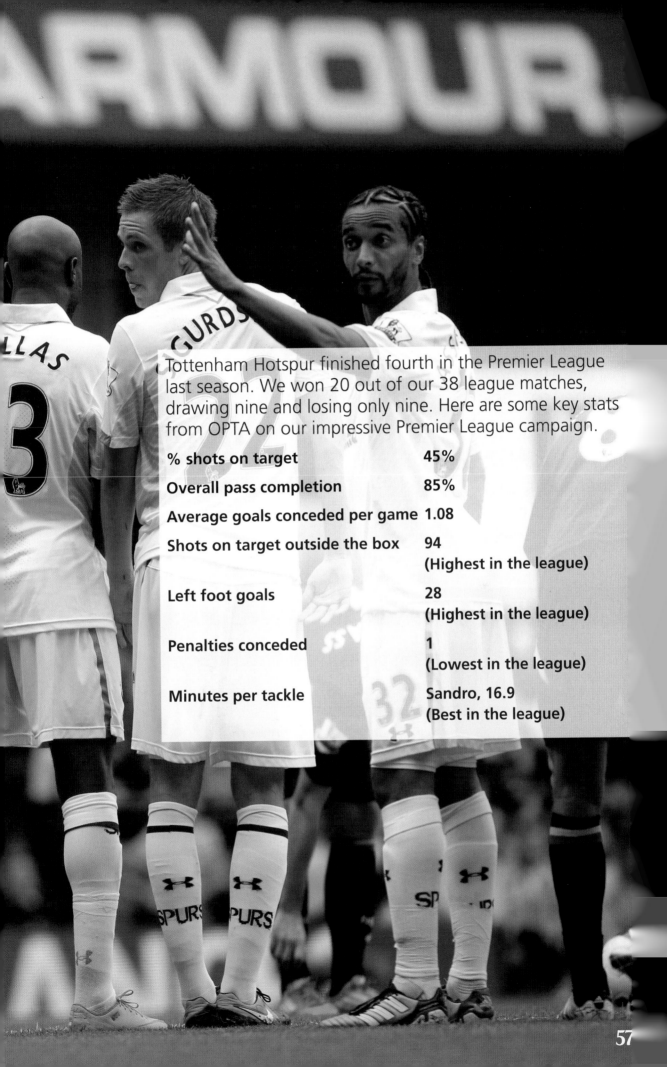

Tottenham Hotspur finished fourth in the Premier League last season. We won 20 out of our 38 league matches, drawing nine and losing only nine. Here are some key stats from OPTA on our impressive Premier League campaign.

% shots on target	45%
Overall pass completion	85%
Average goals conceded per game	1.08
Shots on target outside the box	94 (Highest in the league)
Left foot goals	28 (Highest in the league)
Penalties conceded	1 (Lowest in the league)
Minutes per tackle	Sandro, 16.9 (Best in the league)

TOTTENHAM HOTSPUR
SOCCER SCHOOLS

TOTTENHAM
HOTSPUR
FOOTBALL
DEVELOPMENT

PLAYER DEVELOPMENT COURSES

Learn to play with Tottenham Hotspur and our team of FA/UEFA - qualified coaches.

Come and join us at our Soccer Schools Academy Experiences, Term-Time evening and holiday courses.

FOOTBALL ROADSHOWS

Or come along and test your skills at our popular Spurs Football Roadshows running throughout the year.

SAVE 10% DISCOUNT
WHEN YOU BOOK ONLINE
USE PROMO CODE
"SPURS"

TO BOOK OR FOR MORE INFORMATION:
01. VISIT: tottenhamhotspur.com/soccerschools
02. CALL: 0208 365 5049

TO DARE IS TO DO

QUIZ ANSWERS

P48 SPURS SUPER QUIZ

1. Fourth
2. Newcastle
3. Iceland
4. Chirpy
5. Rubin Kazan, Shamrock Rovers and PAOK
6. Emmanuel Adebayor
7. Nottingham Forest
8. Under Armour
9. European Cup Winners' Cup
10. Steffen Freund
11. West Ham
12. Kyle Walker
13. Four
14. Ajax
15. Newcastle United

P37 WORDSEARCH

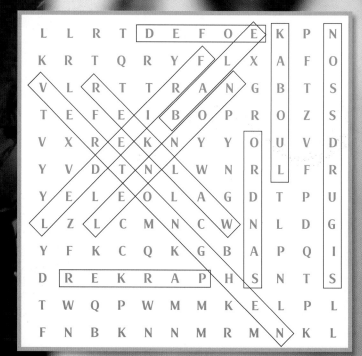

```
L L R T D E F O E K P N
K R T Q R Y F L X A F O
V L R T T R A N G B T S
T E F E I B O P R O Z S
V X R E K N Y Y O U V D
Y V D T N L W N R L F R
Y E L E O L A G D T P U
L Z L C M N C W N L D G
Y F K C Q K G B A P Q I
D R E K R A P H S N T S
T W Q P W M M K E L P L
F N B K N N M R M N K L
```

WHERE'S WALKER...